Beyond

new poems by

ALBERT GOLDBARTH

DAVID R GODINE · PUBLISHER
Boston

First published in 1998 by

DAVID R. GODINE, PUBLISHER, INC.

Box 450

Jaffrey, New Hampshire 03452

Library of Congress Cataloging in Publication Data

Goldbarth, Albert.
    Beyond : poems / by Albert Goldbarth. — 1st ed.
        p.   cm.
    I. Title.
    PS3557.0354B49   1998
    811'.54--DC21   98-35760
                           CIP

ISBN: 1-56792-087-X

First edition, 1998

This book was printed on acid-free paper

Printed in the United States of America

BEYOND

ACKNOWLEDGMENTS

The author is grateful to the editors of the following periodicals, in
which the poems of *Beyond* first appeared.

Agni: "News from Home";
The Beloit Poetry Journal: "Heart on a Chain," "The Two Domains";
Boulevard: "'A Solid is Not Solid'";
The Cream City Review: "Even; Equal";
The Denver Quarterly: "Dolphin in a Zoot Suit";
The Mid-American Review: "Coinages: a fairy tale";
The Ontario Review: "Roses and Skulls," "Meop";
The Paris Review: "Two Cents";
Poetry: "Away," "Thread Through History," "Because It Happened,"
    "Trails of Fire and Spirits," "'A wooden eye...'";
Poetry East: "Across Town";
Poet Lore: "The Red Shift";
Poetry Northwest: "The Winds";
The Western Humanities Review: "Believing a Resonant Chord Exists..."

"Coinages: a fairy tale" was also reprinted in *Harper's*.

In addition, the author thanks Marion Stocking and the editorial staff
    of *The Beloit Poetry Journal* for awarding "The Two Domains" that
    journal's 1994 Chad Walsh Poetry Prize, and for providing a pub-
    lic theatrical reading of that poem—with hats.

Thanks, too, to the Center for the Study of Science Fiction for select-
    ing "The Two Domains" as its 1995 Theodore Sturgeon Memorial
    Award for Best Science Fiction Story of the Year, Special Category.

And entrepreneurial thanks to Jim Wolken of Skinner-James.

Disembodied; infinite; borderless; fogborne; apparition;
transcendence—these are my passwords.

half of the time we're gone
but we don't know where
and we don't know where

–Paul Simon

CONTENTS

Introduction

HEART ON A CHAIN

"The spirits of the dead"—it's important to specify,
there are *so* many others. Among the islands, spirits
of water and coral. For the mountain tribes, the wind
is a spirit, it bombasts as it polishes the high passes.
But it's the risen spark and semblance of the dead
that rides us intimately, that squats with us
inside whatever's the privatemost hole of our day.
They can offer advice—the gone, the revenant-ones—
or terrify: in Chaco tribes, the kin
of the newly dead take new names, hoping so to sidle
from the specter's wrathful notice. In the oldest caves
we habited are painted rounds of the wall rock that
were interdimensional talkspots, where we asked and
where the ancestors answered. / She

presides over "detail lab" for Cave A-32.
Somebody else unearths—a shovel and a sifter.
She unparticles that earth—sometimes refining it
to one resilient donkey hair she'll work across
a shard of human bone, dislodging 30,000 years of burial
grain by grain. Her task as the grant defines it is this
exactly and only: "initial detail rendering of osseous finds."
But how *not* to refit them in her mind?—to string
the butterflies of bone they duly bring her
into vertebrae again; and then enflesh the life,
its woes and thrivings, back around that
recharged chord. They all have highbrow Ph.D.'s; and
even so, she knows their secret pleasure is that of the parlor
seance: saying *yes* to ectoplasm. / This

is the couple she oftenest reconstructs: the hunt
is done for the day, a last fresh axe-head hafted
with the clan's last pliant vine... and now they rest on a ledge
together, these two, and watch the limestone distance darken
gradually... this "proto-us," and their various proto
-yearnings and -uneases, -suspicions, -sweetnesses
...see?: we can't escape recasting them familiarly,
the baleful shades of Homer, as well as the homier
conjured spinster aunts and prelates of Victorian mediums, all
are necessarily envisioned in a version
of the tropes we live out daily; and
the truth is, we're *their* archeological study in a way,
the past they're drawn to, visit, sift, and even speak to,
in their former language: throat and tooth and tongue... / She

!ooga! she *!ooga!*——the weekly mail-&-sundries jeep
pops all of them out of their Paleolithic reveries, with
Thrilling Goodies From Home to thin the thickly solitary
drudge of fieldwork. Well, not for her this week
or the last or the one before. Her first month here, he sent
an antique locket——tiny heart tipped with a breath-thin chain——or
someone had: no note. This absence follows her
through her days of caves and tagged shin fragments
so outrageously faithfully, it *is* a presence, one
the very blankness of which prohibits hurt or disappointment:
these require detail. Is she comforted?——yesno.
One day behind the quonset hut she saw two bugs attached
in fucking; *no*, she saw, she looked again: one was dead,
a husk, and the other was stuck to it, was dragging it. / He

walks the pier in Portland, *ambles* really, breathing in
the ocean air that so revivifies his soul but can
corrode a u.s. battleship. Now this is his life, his
therapy: and every breath, on better days, erases
the faces that, hobgoblinlike, torment his sleep
—his parents ringed in fire
like some hellish circus act; as for the ex-wife
and the kids and what once happened, well... enough
of that. And as for Miss Bones Digger-Upper, he
hopes she understood the love in making a gift
of his grandmother's pendant. One day he'll be
"fully in the present tense again," then he'll
get on with "the flow of the moment." For now...
so many ghosts to lay to rest.

SLOUGHED BODIES

THE RED SHIFT

...he loved not Fish, John Aubrey writes,
though borne in a Fish-towne. Somewhere

in the heartland, a man is looking out his window
at the early light that's almost solid,

something burnished, standing there in the wheat...
You know it's not just that we're born,

but that we're born *away from* someone.
The entire universe everywhere in its every part

is *away*—including its people parts.
He sips his morning coffee; soon

he'll walk down to the brook, to bathe...
its water roughly scrubbed over his skin...

fifteen years, and he still thinks the stink
of cod and herring is in him.

AWAY

We think a blink is tiny but
it's the size of all of our eyelashes, it's
the length of the drop of a meteor
that could rub out City Hall
and melt a mile circle of asphalt, so
like any of the body's several hundred taken-for-granted
accordion-pleatings, slinks, and spatula-flips, a blink
says a brachiate maze of human evolution going back
past protozoa, and also says, the way the shrilling voice
of a fallopian tube or the prostate will, that pain enough
to fell us like a hammer can fit on a pin.
If *that's* the standard, the eyelashes come to look
as large as a row of hussar swords uplifted in a toast.
If that's the standard, no wonder a blink is span aplenty
for the cockroach on the kitchen floor to vanish
without so much as even a hokey, magicianly poof
—to vanish, waving its own two perfect lashes that,
for all I know, detected the landing thump of Viking I on Mars
before it registered with NASA. Of course entire people disappear:
what genocide is all about; and also entire cities: Tikál,
Ixkún, Flores, Palenque, and the temple center of Copán,
all abandoned by the ancient Maya, given over
to jungle creeper and thorny furze
completely, like an origami metroplex undoing itself
not only back to paper but back
beyond that to the wild paper reeds. To the stones,
the god-faced Mayan stones, this
would have happened in the blink of an eye,
a stone's eye. But tonight I don't mean anything
that vast, I only mean my friend Dolores says
she turns these days to Eduardo in bed and sees
he's someone else—the man she married seven years ago

has been replaced by a figure of balsa and wax,
a *perfect* likeness, but a likeness none the less.
And the department of stats confirms this: each year,
thousands of wives and husbands put on parkas and go
inside of themselves, they say for a pack of cigarettes, and go
up in smoke. It happens. Who *hasn't*
lit the overheads suddenly onto some marriage and seen it
scuttle under the bed or behind the heirloom platter,
blasted out of the real world of community, into cockroach space?
The delights of Away are many. The grass of Away
is a deeper, sweeter, narcotic viridian than the lawns of Here
could ever be fertilized into. O write me c/o Vamoose,
Oblivion. When I was a child,
six or seven or so, and the day was six or seven thousand
consecutive terrors and humiliations, and everything spun
too fast to grasp exactly, including love, including self,
I'd curl in bed—the way I might now,
or my wife might now, although with the return half
of the ticket in our holding—and my lids would close
(those Roman galleys fitted out with oars),
would take me into the night, down the flow and the beat,
would row me away on the black sea
of that disappearing ink.

What is it, what *really* is it, this sacred or secular
aurochs on the cave wall, with its great horns
nearly as circular as the full moon, and a swag of paint
that forms the haunch so thickly-laid it speaks
of the kind of delicious fat that rivers over your jaws
with the richness of living animal coursing inside it?
This beak-headed shaman (if it's a shaman),
this globular goddess (if it's a goddess)—what
are they? In ancient Greece, they'd ask the god
for help in mending this or that infirmity
—they'd spend a night on the sanctuary floor
while the tame snakes slithered and licked
medicinally—and sometimes they would bring
a small clay model of the afflicted part: intestines
looking like small clay snails; starry clay hands.
The healing springs of Vicarello, near Rome,
have yielded over 1500 coins to our archeological
sifting of their undermucks: and in the knowingly
gnomish gloom of a tourist trap called Santa's Village
I once saw a boy, about seven, let a penny
down the dark of a mossily picturesque well
with his eyes scrunched into a dire longing,
yes, and his lips in motion as if trying somehow
to give a voice to the overpresiding spirit of the place
—as if belief could be a form of karaoke.
I remember passing on the way back
one of those seemingly helterskelter neighborhoods of trailer homes
in the middle of what was otherwise Midwest dust
to the horizon. At the front of one, a woman
was beating the ground with a broken golf club,
beating it ceaselessly and vigorously with a violent persistence
that crazily had such a purity to it,

such a weird integrity, the motion transported her
onto another level of being. In back, a man, I imagine
the husband, stared from a window
with eyes as widely empty as dishes the cats licked clean
—whatever was in those eyes to begin with,
beaming past the moon by now.
There are *many* names for this, psychological,
sociological names.
But I know wishing when I see it.

TWO CENTS

Academia 1994: these dead white males
I've been hauling about in this brick of a box of a book
called *Western Civilization*—Homer, Plato, Melville,
and the rest of the Anglo-Sultans of Civ.—have
seemingly weighted me down: at least, I'm told so.
I shake the book; I hear the rattle
of its ponderous Goliath beetles of history,
while elsewhere someone holds a copy of something like
New Rainbows: Multi-Voices, and
its ladybugs and mayflies lightly hum and lift
their reader into higher realms of consciousness,
as if the neocortex were merely another layer
of gray, confining atmosphere to rise above.
Goodbye, goodbye, I heavily wave. That's

one example. Another—a friend confides: the woman
she calls her "female mentor" (a lauded lit-crit doyenne
exemplary at both oracular wisdom and daintier,
humbler, daily graces) suddenly hemorrhaged and
two hours after that died: "and on her deathbed
told me, I guess by way of finally cleaning
every interior surface, that she'd once done something,
I won't say what, but something, *so* demeaning
involving this man she knew to be completely meretricious,
and yet... Well, what I'm saying is, that's
two deaths. First, the person I *thought* she was, died;
then she died in her wholeness. Now... how can I say it?
She left 'us'... *incomplete*, and so I carry her everywhere,
invisibly, my osteoporotic hump, my camelback, whispering to me."

Examples swarm me: D-Day's 50th anniversary, and
the local paper rehashes the Japanese soldier

found on that island twenty years after the War, still
loyal to Hirohito and armed with a bayonet. The man
who weeps for the fallen Führer. The woman whose self
is predicated on membership in D.A.R.—who
harnesses herself every morning, and all day drags
the Mayflower in her wake. Or this: "I know by now
how tired a cliché it is, but, hey: my father drank,
I drink"—and then the long tale of DNA in a gene pool
spiked like a frat party punch. The truth is: everybody
alive is small against the dead,
in ways sustaining and misshaping simultaneously.
A favorite page in *Western Civilization* tries

describing Rome in 1100: cowherds and rush-weavers
living amid the abandoned grandeur, patching huts together
of mud and thatch inside the walls of public buildings
—temples, garrisons, arenas—so unthinkably vast,
the work of gods or demons, they were seen as plains
and mountainridge escarpments. Huts
against those columns like lesions on bones. And
life, of course, unceasingly buzzing in each of them:
a cooking-stone; a sexual musk; a hide to soften. . . .
I also think of a tale I've read of two wanderers
who sheltered overnight in a magical cave the fates
provided: the skull of a whale Time had worn clean,
into a fabulous sanctum. Huddled all night, in its head,
like a thought, like two cents clinking together.

COINAGES: A FAIRY TALE

On May 1, 1947, when *airlift* barely existed, my father
lay down beside my mother. He wasn't my father
yet, she wasn't my mother, not technically, the late sun
played the scales of light on the lake at Indian Lodge State Park,
and *rocket-booster* was new by a year, and *thruway*
only by two, and *sputnik* waited somewhere
in the clouded-over swales of the future and, beyond it,
pixel, rolfing, homeboy, floated
in a *cyberspace* too far-removed and conceptual
even to be defined by cloud. He stroked her. She stirred
in her veil of slumber—when was the last time
anyone "slumbered," except in a poem?—but didn't wake.
Not that he wanted to wake her: only to stay
in contact with this singular, corporeal thing they'd made
of themselves amid the chenille and gas heat of the room.
It would be night soon. It would be dusk, and then
the dreamy, let's say the oneiric, nighttime.
Macrobiotic would come into being, *fractal, rock-and-roll*.
The first reported use of *twofer, LP, fax* is 1948.
Spelunker, 1946, and *cybernetics, TV, vitamin B-12*, were
newfangled, still as if with the glister
of someone's original utterance on them. Others,
say, the *kit bag* that they'd lazily left open near the radio, as in
"pack up your troubles in your ol' kit bag and smile,
darn you, smile"—were even now
half-insubstantial, like a remnant
foxfire glimmering richly over a mound of verbal mulch.
Wingding, riffraff, tittle-tattle: holding even. I'm not saying
vocabulary is people, or anything easily
equational like that—although surely
we've all known a generation going *naught* and *o'er* and *nary*
that disappeared with its language. How

was the pulse of *boogie-woogie* doing? *demesne? lapsarian?*
He looked out the window—as solid by now with darkness
as a tile trivet. Obsidian. Impenetrable.
He looked *at* it—or *through* it—or looked crystal ball-like *into* it
at himself, and tried to practice things he'd been wanting to say.
Outside, in an invisible ripple, *eleemosynary* faded
further from the fundament of human use—and *farrier*
and *haberdasher* and *lyre* and *tocsin* and *arras* and *yore*.
When was the last time a liar dissembled, the cressets were lit,
the nefarious were vilified? My father said "Albert"
—that was the name they'd decided on, for a boy. He breathed it
into the night, into the turning invisible
bingo drum of give-and-take out there, where *radar* was new
and dynastic, and *transistor* was equally sturdy,
and *aerosporin*, and the brave new world of *xerox* and *laser* and *virtual
    reality*
held initiating breath in abeyance, somewhere
yonder in future time. "Albert"—it had been his father's name.
My mother opened her eyes now, she was sprawled in a daringly
    brief,
but sensibly flannel, nightie—exactly
under the ceiling fan, that turned like the oars of rowers
who keep circling over some fabulous discovery below.
That's what my father thought: it was fabulous! *They*
were fabulous! And he was terrified,
too; he knew that over the dark hills in the dark night,
varlets waited, and scurrilous knaves, and goons and racketeers,
he knew the darkness spewed forth villainy and predation the way
a spoiled cheese frothed maggots—after all,
he'd searched out bodies in the coal mine
with a thin wood lathe they'd issued him for feeling through
the seepage, and he'd lounged around the poolrooms
where the ward boss and his thick, pomaded cronies
held their shabby court. By this, and by the other signs

a body ages into itself, he understood the emptiness
in everything, he understood it long before
neutrino and *pulsar* and *chaos theory* would be
the current buzz, and simply standing there
in his half-price Florsheim wingtip brogues he'd polished
to an onyx shine, he understood a man and a woman
clatter for the casual amusement of the gods
like pea gravel flung in an oil drum. All this,
and a sense of grandiosity, of flame and aching sweetness
in the coils of him, and of the Milky Way he'd touched increasingly
alive in her skin... all this, and more, was asking him, now,
to be brought into speech, on May 1, 1947,
at Indian Lodge State Park. He swallowed,
and was silent, and shook, until she saw
and asked what was the matter.
He didn't have the words.

EVEN; EQUAL

Snow all night. It fills whole gullies
as easily as sidewalk cracks.
Finally, nothing has definition.
Last winter, at the first real thaw,
they found two schoolgirls under half-receded ice,
the bruises frozen
into lustrous brooches at their frozen throats.
Whoever did it is out here still, is free and maybe
needing more. The word "injustice" doesn't include
the choking gall that burns through me—something like being
here tonight, at my father's grave,
where even the shitty winter weather seems to fall
in the white weave of those off-the-rack, sagged suits
he wore so a few saved dollars could buy my education.
On the cemetery's other side, the tailored graves
of college deans and oil barons. What do I know?
Maybe he's playing poker with them
all night tonight, while January piles up
in deep banks, and the elements
of their own sloughed bodies skirl and reshuffle.
Death—the way snow makes the ditch
and the window sill even; equal.

A death-cry ripens, and rises—a boy's,
a seven-year-old's—and holds within itself,
as if we couldn't have guessed, the whole
of an adult yearning to remain attached
at the root, and the crotch, and the tongue-bud's stem,
among the desires of *this*
imperfect world. A seven-year-old, and a fever
he's exiting through. He's brought to moan and dwindle,
on a softly woven pallet reserved for the sick,
in a room that opens onto the water. The room
itself has been done by an artisan in the typical frieze
of vaguely wave- or shell-like spirals
at top and bottom of all three major walls
—this is one of the ancient world's sea-kingdoms.
The boy, his mother: so still,
they might have been done by the artisan, too.
She's kneeled, she bends above him
with such concentrative force, we see it
the way we would in expressionist painting: now
how the walls, and the hint outside of clouds,
and the room, and the darkening daylight, *everything*
is bending pliantly over his wasting form.
My point is: we'll see it again,
this picture. It's one of the well-known few that won't stop
reappearing in the species' continuity: this small,
familial lamentation. Here it is,
a slowly opened flower of paternal scream
as stones are placed on the eyes of the three-month-old,
and a sheep's-teat suckle-bag positioned at its right side,
and a cow horn on its left, and then the whole assemblage
lowered down the arid, yellowed foothills earth
of the Tian Shan, the "Celestial Mountains," nearly

2,000 years ago. Here it is in 1910, a luckless Russian *shtetl*,
as a sister feeds a sister—watered milk
sopped up a twist of rag—her final meal. But
let me add that over an arm of the inlet,
in another spiral-decorated room, the coming smudge of dusk
upon the sun-shot water means that oil is being decanted
into a hundred roughly-done clay lamps:
their light will soon be dappling on the masked and dancing whirl
of wedding revelers—that other
repetitive scene in the human annals.
                                        All this
sweeps through me unbidden as I sit in Bōnz
(a hoity-toity rib joint, where your mouth gets halo'd saucy
while a harpist in the corner works intently at her instrument).
I'm in a booth, across from Mommy Fannie,
Auntie Hannah, Auntie Sally (total age,
240 years; combined height, 15 feet). They're one
three-headed mythological lady-beast: the Muse
of Free-Association Family History, and its ever-recessive
fractal'ed reach through time. "No, Hannah:
don't be silly. Fay died *after* Helen moved to California,
didn't she, Sally?" "After, *of course*. Because
she wasn't at Beverly's wedding, and" *counterpointing
this with a breadstick* "that's! how! I! know!"
"Do they give you more rolls if you ask?" "Do *I* know? *Ask.*"
"'Ask.' I asked for more butter when the salads came…"
holding forth the butter dish incriminatingly "…SO?"
"In San Diego I go with friends to a restaurant, Tessie's,
Bessie's, something, they have rolls there, I tell you
you have to tie a string to them like with balloons, they're so light."
A one-pulse silence. "Albie… you remember Fay?"
                                        I don't
remember Fay. "When we were children together,
seven, eight, her younger brother died—you should listen

to this, because it happened—I say 'younger,' an *infant*,
still at the breast. And we were so poor, a coffin
cost so much. And the grownups, they were talking about it,
what to do, a commotion, crying, nobody knew, and Fay
—I'll never forget this—went up to her mother, *Tantë* Ruthie,
with a paper box her doll had come in, 'Mommy,'
she said" *my mother weeping over an empty butter dish*
"'can you use this?'"
                        When I tell you
that a vaguely wave- or shell-like spiral
opens in the restaurant air, I mean
that from the center of her harp, a woman,
with both hands,
traces the shape of a chambered nautilus.

"A SOLID IS NOT SOLID

but chiefly holes. If we could empty the emptiness
out of an elephant it would shrink to much less
than the size of a mouse." And we would be left with
…what? the pill of an elephant; its -ness.
And even this, of course, is subatomic pixels
of the periodic table, that have come here from the stars
and the lime-rich rains and the undersea teeth
of an *earlier* universe, and might have just as well become
that sleepy, sated sexual thing
between your own legs, after love one evening
——less than the size of a mouse. "Each dot
can take its part in endless different images—perhaps one second
a cow and the next a speedboat": John McCrone
on the constituency of a TV image. After love

one evening, after even the after-love TV winks dead,
he studies the woman asleep a hand-width away and
wonders at how this thing they've called an "us," and that
he once thought of as statuary—something like a shape
of them in granite—turns out, over the years, to breathe
and whicker and moult, to be a live thing of its own,
in a mutation of itself compounded daily.
There's a wry cartoon by Charles Addams: a wife
in bed, with her back to the bed's other side, and saying
"…and don't think I don't know you're lying there
wishing you were with someone else." The other side
of the bed is empty; a bat is flying out the blackly open
bedroom window. "Everybody changes"—that's
what he thinks; while she, on the other hand, thinks

——there isn't any "other hand," though; there's only
the patterned sprinkle of what we are, inside a matrix

that will make of us a thousand other patterns. In a poem
composed of *this* poem's few components rearranged,
she's watching *him* asleep. The lamplight puddles over
the book in her lap, and leaves him
—only inches over—in an insulating dimness. Who
is he, *what* is he, *now,* when the brain rolls over in sleep
to let the darkness stroke its underbelly?... Questions
even the Great and Gone Ones never answered. She turns to her
   book.
It's Dickens. Mr. Micawber is speaking: "Gentlemen,
do with me as you will! I am straw upon the surface
of the deep, and am tossed in all directions by the elephants
—I beg your pardon, I should have said the elements."

In his comic books' chimeric air, a doorslam
makes a visible series of ripples
shake the house. That's how he draws it,
in his room now, with his gush-of-tears held back
in anger. *Feeding* on the anger: he's a fire
ravenous over a page, a notebook page
—this eight-year-old. This sketcher and schemer.
Well maybe *they* should be on fire: the father

he draws with licks of wild lion's-mane-like flame
around his gumball of a head, and the mother
runs across the page's whiteness arson'ed
neck-to-toe, as if she wears a sheet of Hell itself
for an evening gown. There's even
the magical feel that drawing it *causes* it,
that upstairs in their bedroom they really are
roaring like two great trashfires in the night, and

if not, then maybe at least a searing pain
about the size of a zipper-pull
ignites inside their chests for just the flick of time
it would take a Zippo to burn someone then be snapped off,
why not?—through middle childhood
the increasing assurance that something(-body) "out of sight"
maintains somewhere its independent being
is an understanding increasingly

("gotcha!") refined and exploited. This is the science
of voodoo dolls as well—and though we call these
"mumbojumbo" condescendingly, we still stare
at the wall-length map (with crimson pins
for each successful business franchise stippling it

manifest-destinywise) and find ourselves believing,
in some moss-grown, remnant brain node, that the map is actively
generative of conquest. More appealing

an example is the travel (in units of miniature
cornflour footprints) up the axial "Pollen Way"
in a traditional Navajo sand painting: over
a set amount of days, the patient is represented
as journeying through this square, with "Big Fly,"
"Little Wind," the twofold "Spirit Bringers,"
and the pantheonic rest, until a healing
of the body is effected. Of Jackson Pollock

in 1943: "...he felt the need to heal himself,
and he felt that since Paris, the former
world art center, had been overtaken by Nazis,
he had to go back to the beginning of art
—to Navajo sand paintings..." —this,
as context for the twizzling, rhythmic stride
of almost-figures in his twenty-foot-long *Mural*. When
Ginsberg writes "I declare the war in Vietnam over!"

—*is* it over? in the "real world"? or in the poet's own
apocalyptic and love-marbled heart? I don't know.
What I do know: there's an eight-year-old,
his day's splenetic rages eased by venting them
in emulation of just these open comic book pages
surrounding his sleep (he sleeps now): people
superturning into live infernos, superflying
over spooky moonscapes, superbestialpowering themselves,

because our insides *do* such things, while on the outside we
survive another twenty-four hours of simple goodjoe citizenship,
or try to. In these last eight lines, I'd like to think

he's peaceful; that, upstairs, they're sleeping peacefully
amid the cooled-down ashes of parental ire; and
also that you, approaching the finish, will think of this
writing as something that's manipulated you safely
through trails of damaging fire and spirit bringers.

These are the nights when I think of the housemaid
cleaning that woman's cubby. First
she empties the basin of water and the chamberpot.
Then she returns, the sheets as usual are caked
with use, and these she changes, making sure
the new sheets like the old ones have a lace hem.
Under the bed, amid a circus of shoes,
of Roman sandals, and saucy mules, and furled Oriental slippers,
she finds the packet tied in twine, which she undoes
and, after the first brute shock, removes
the ear. She holds it in her palm
until it looks just like her palm, but swirled a little.
The whorls have brittled, and the lobe is blue
with paint, from where he tugged at it, in thought,
while working, listening hard to the cry in the wood
and the cloth and the plate and the night winds.

BELIEVING A RESONANT CHORD EXISTS BETWEEN HIS WORK AND THE WORLD, PIETER BRUEGEL ATTEMPTS TO HELP BANISH THE TARANTELLA

> *One dancing epidemic began in the Nether-*
> *lands.... Some towns banished the colour*
> *red, or pointed shoes, on the grounds that*
> *these brought on the seizures.*
> —Michell and Rickard, *Phenomena*

As to the whale's gullet I have been pleased to paint
spread open as red as childbirth
in the milky-green violent waters,
as red as the rooster's comb or the cat's inflamed ass-petals
—though the striking of its colors took me
out of this vale of haggling and pox for a moment, still
I bid that fishy, fleshy sleeve of unrepentant redness
be sewn closed,
a bag of mottled gray-and-violet in the waves. And
I consign this plate of cherries to the fire.
I consign the fire to *its* fire, let it be eaten
into whatever invisibility precedes and long outlives
what we call "flames." The lavish depicting of Hell
has kept me steady company on otherwise drearisome days,
and yet I ask that the red of its torments
and the blood-red of its devils' rigid members
and the rouge-red of its sassier delights
ascend in the colors of char, to the white clouds
in the blue sky, and disperse there.
And the homespun reds of shawls and codpieces.
The butcherblock's red. The red on the sheets
of the marriage-bed in the morning. I say:
begone! The gorge the slain boar leaves,
like burn marks, trailed into the snow: away!

The red of tripe, with purple stars in it.
The web in the wearied eye.
And the red of soldiers' coats I've threaded
through the five hundreds of onlookers scattered
over my largest, my brutal and lovely
Procession to Calvary, and so by this you trace to where
a figure in the clutter kneels under the weight of his cross...
reravel this red to a red knot, snip it out of the scene
and its history. Here a flower,
there a smeary dawn—these, also, I consign
to the ravenous maw of redness
and I command that maw to swallow itself
into slate, into sand, into celadon.
Even the tawnier reds: fox skins, expensive woods.
Even the red in pink nipples.
And as to the pointed shoes—likewise!

✳

She kicks her ruby patent leather fuck-me's off
in the same smooth move that knees the front door shut.
They pinch her harder than a beer-breath lech and
some days she could gladly flay those heels with a razor,
wishing both alive enough to wince in pain—but
then again, she knows, they help arrange her
lavish physiognomy into just the right tippable look,
and not just dollar tips, one regular slips
a twenty up her garter for each of three songs in the set.
That's belly-bang music, she calls it. What
she turns on now, once the residue jangle dims down
in her head, is the same mellifluous Tchaikovsky

>   *because someone is weeping, dramatically*
>   *holding her own head like a damaged pet*

—someone else, somewhere, is sitting calmly
in wafers of afternoon light that sprinkle
down from an elm, just sitting there
in the lull between two pleasures

she ballet'd to as a child, and now drags Sammi,
six, to class to ballet to, as well. *To tutu to,*
she says, and pours herself a generous gin and lemon.
Outside, the light at the start of this one more day is also
clear, with citrus. She thinks of the shrinking looks
the other mothers give when she walks in—as if she were
catching. As if to dance a sassy tarantella of lust
for fun and profit erases her out of the world
of supermarkets, PTA, small courtesies. Over
42 million dollars are spent for admission to nude bars
every week—not tips, just basic cover charge—but no one
wants two cents of her at the Parish Bazaar. Well

because someone is joyous, throwing
great rays of desirability over a room
—someone, somewhere else, is mourning,
is banded in black crepe, perfectly
still and remembering love
as if through turbid water

the hell with that anyway, right? It's "night"
for her—it's 8 a.m.; she thinks *Because they're happy...*
falling into sleep beneath a poster of his frantic, packed
The Wedding Dance. Because someone is marrying, someone
in another painting is walking on stumps. Because somebody
is an entomologist tweezing a living dot into the light,
somebody else is resolving the orbits of planets. Because
this happens, that doesn't. Listen.... Quiet.... You can hear
the Possible issue its tiny cries at the edge

of our actual world. Because somebody's dancing,
somebody isn't: somebody's *painting* dancing, in a room,
in a mood, in a head-encircling cloud of linseed and solitude.

✳

> 1. *All languages contain terms for white and*
>   *black (light shades and dark shades)*
> 2. *If a language contains three terms for colors,*
>   *then it contains a term for red.*
> > —the first 2 of 7 "color levels,"
> > Berlin and Kay, *Basic Color Terms*

The design isn't working. Somewhere,
an imperfectly attended-to detail leans
awry, he knows this, and he stands there in the unrelenting
northern light, that won't be fooled or say a canted thing
is straight; he stands in that revealing field and knows
the design isn't working but doesn't know where.
The poisonman easily swinging a leather strap of a dozen rats?
The trestle table piled high in gobbets of ox and pancakes?
The haymow? The bagpipes player? The shadow of a bird,
by which we see how still the water?... He doesn't
know; and so he starts to nude this, layer, layer, back
until its flaw is uncovered. Purple goes (the artery,
for instance, in the stretched throat of the hog, and the glint
in the blade against that pulse) and so the seventh level
disappears and, in it, orange, pink and gray.
Then the brown of the omelette vendor's daughter's eyes;
and the mange-hound's shit; and the softer-than-fawn
in the dove, at dusk, against the gnarl of its chosen bole;
and so the sixth level. Each, in turn—until
this sixteenth century *ur*-x-ray
of his Netherlandish scene at level one:

a peopled world of only
bone, and the darkness where no bone is;
of axe-edged silver moonlight, and shadow;
of ice, and coal; of milk, and ink;
of bridal lace, and the grave.
Inside a silence as stark as this duochrome world,
he studies its essential undergraining... *here,*
and *here....*
                    And then a wail
breaks through Pieter Bruegel's window: pain,
perhaps, or sexual fervor... and he begins the slow,
gradationed recompletion of his universe.
Level two. They're dancing, in red.
Who is he to stop them?

"Jee-ZUSS, I just got a call from the crazy old bitch,
she bought herself a shotgun, a *shotgun*, now
if Vessie ever tries climbing back in the house she says
she's going to blow his balls off—look, I've got to go
sort this out for them, do you want to come too?"
I've only known Joan a week. A week. Now Vessie
does a crow-dance on my shoulder, and nutty Irene
on the other. A trailer they've painted in roses and skulls.
"I've never told you… when these things happen I
turn on almost everyone I love. (*pause*) Will you hold me?"

Really entering another's life…?—is like you're walking through
the flat and familiar background of thirteenth-century paintings
when, with a sickening whoosh, perspective
gets invented; and the world, its saints (with halos
like those crimped gold-foil paper cups
for gourmet chocolates), its shitdump-guzzling swine,
its finches and beggars' bells and candelabra, *everything*,
is tumbled and sucked down the colonnade lines to a pinhole
on the horizon, as if a bullethole opened up in the shell
of a jetliner, and you're lost lost lost. Disorienting

switches in style, though, are nothing compared to switches
in world-view. If this "person" from a 1580 folk-art painting
steps inside this Impressionist day in a sun-emblazoned hillscape:
he's a "child," "childhood" having been invented by now. Or
move this houndsteeth streak of mountains, Romantically
rendered as glorious, back one hundred years: and it's
a bleak impediment to travel, only that. In Lucas Cranach's
Staghunt (1544), the splendid ladies of the court row out
to watch the great beasts disembowled by dogs, an afternoon's
diversion: run *that* past your Sensitivity Workshop. Zapping

back-and-forth between two worlds accumulates
a dangerous static charge along the zapline, and is never
as easy as s-f adventures imply with their casual *pop*
of inter-time or -dimensional travel. Wife and husband
dunk each other lustily in the tub, then transact
business from it: this is a Medieval painting—master,
mistress, seven children, four apprentices, several poor relations,
and a scurry of servants live in these two hall-like, straw-strewn rooms
of a standard bourgeois house, where tables are also beds and
sleep six visitors at a time, *our* sense of "privacy" not

existing yet. For that, we need to enter this
mid-sixteenth-century Dutch home, brick and gabled, where a couple,
for the first time, is a "couple," defined by surrounding
intimate buffer-space. The architecture says this: *snug*
is Dutch in origin. Bickering. Planning. Waking
like two elements in suspension, in their own and conspired
suspension. Having "psychologies." Knickknacks. Pulling up
into the trailer court's lot: "Oh I didn't tell you anything about Angelo;
no matter what he says, *agree.*" As if holding your own face woefully
in your hands at midnight isn't enough. Now holding this other face.

MEOP

I.

The scenario is: I'm six, and an invincible Venusian army of robots
swarms the city, easily conquering its human defenders with (guess what)
death rays shooting like 1954 home-movie-projector lightbeams
out of their boxy heads, in *Target Earth*. In *Devil Girl from Mars*,
the eponymous leather-fetishy siren of outer space attacks
accompanied by Chani, stomping hunk-o'-hardware robot
extraordinaire, whose particular laser-like sizzle disintegrates
a tree, a barn, a village truck, and a villager. No oratory
dissuades these invaders, no pitiable stare. And if this
somehow all sounds comic in my cavalier retelling, I
assure you it wasn't, then—no, it was set to exactly
my level of terror then. We're born instinctively knowing
an enemy awaits us, and the world provides it a series of faces
keyed to match our ageing understandings. Though there's also Tobor
   (robot

backwards), he of 1954's *Tobor the Great:* playpal of the movie's
plucky eleven-year-old kid-star "Gadge," and rescuer of the boy
from threatened tortures at the hands of foreign spies
(of the kind who speak like ziss, and hiss and glower).
The lesson is: of every order of being, there must be
nemesis and hero, in a tug-of-warring balance. Satan
predicates St. Michael, and vice-versa: they
require one another. Yes, but how to tell? The neighbor-lady
led away one afternoon by a county official
for holding her daughter's open palm against the flat of an iron
"so she'd listen good..." spoke not one hokey ziss or zat to flag
her culpability. I knew about the moon's dark side:
aliens' secret bases were there. But what about people?
—what about inside? what about simple earthly night?

2.

The fabled Kansas flatness seems to go so far, we *couldn't*
be the same "us" by the time we've finally exited its distance.
When I drive this wheaten vastity, I see how life is space
enough for each of us to segue through a programmed range
of consecutive selves, some less than what we'd wish for, some
so seemingly "other" we shiver in our passage. And that Shiva
the Destroyer, and Shiva the Dancer of Life, are one—is just
a mythic hyperstatement of whatever robot/tobor me-*du-jour* we
carry confusingly into the lives of those we love (see
Paramount's 1958 *I Married a Monster from Outer Space*).
My wife's in bed tonight with a novel in which one brother becomes
a ruthless mafioso, one a priest. And then she sleeps,
whoever she is in her recombinant life, while I'm up
writing, whoever I am. Sometimes I think of Skyler

and myself: a car is driving through the lengthways Kansas landscape
like some blip on an ongoing medical read-out, everyone hoping
it stays within the central "steady-state" for soma
and psyche, but sometimes it peaks off toward the edges.
Then, whatever (even ordinary) patience we can summon
is required, or it thins into ire; or infrastructures itself
into something amazingly like forgiveness. Just last night
I turned in bed to see us both awash in moonlight
made so jittered by the stir of nearby trees, it looked
as if we gave off semaphore—although the message
might have come from Alpha Centauri, for all I understood it.
Her face went visible, then guarded; clear, then variegated
weirdly. All night, both of us: a flickered glimpse of beings
from the lunar dark side. Trebla. Relyks.

"A wooden eye. An 1884 silver dollar. A homemade explosive. A set of
false teeth. And a 14-karat gold ashtray,"

says my wife, and then she looks up from her book
called something like *Cockamamie Facts* and tests me:
"What's their common denominator?"—right. As if
we still believe some megamatrix substrate (God,
or atoms, or Imagination) holds the infinite unalike dots
of *its* body in a parity, and daily life reflects this. As if
all of our omniform, far-post-lungfish, nuttier-than-Boschian
evolution, crowned by any ten minutes of channel-surfing
the news and (little difference) entertainment possibilities here
at the bung-end of the millennium, hadn't knocked that idea
out of our heads and onto what my father would have charmingly called
its bazoonkus. Common denominator—sure. And yet

it's Sunday night—my wife is reading in bed, with the grim
conviction that the work-week upcoming is going to be one
spirit-dead, hellacious spate of days—and so her mood,
her mind, increasingly assume the über-darkness of the night
itself, the way "industrial melanization" means those moths
in the factory districts gradually blackened to match
their new, soot/city background: and I see, now, how
the sleepless nun, and the lycanthrope in a skulking prowl,
and the warehouse watchman telling the face of his friend
the clock his griefs, his griefs... are all subsumed and
equalized into the night, as into a magpie's hoard: so
maybe some Ultracommodiousness, some Great Coeval, does

exist (it might be the Night, it might be almost any of our
pancultural abstractions) and welcomes us into its organizational
gestalt. If so... if so, it's more than *my* day's scan
of newspaper cullings and letters can ever rise above itself
to see. I learn someone's investigated the annual global methane emission

in cattle gas; that every seven years a god will fill the toad
attached to the tip of a ritual ribboned pole, and glow like a lamp
in its warty belly—then it rains; that only yesterday a girl,
eleven, was found with the name of a rival gang, the *Lady Satans*,
carefully cut in her thigh and rubbed with drainpipe acid. Somewhere
there may be a world where such as these are equally legitimized, but
not here in the thick and swirling mists of Planet Albert. So

imagine my confusion today at a letter from friend Alane,
who's sweet enough to read and like my poems, and praises
my "inclusiveness," and writes "I'm watching a man with nothing
below the waist on television. He's saying he can do anything.
He walks on his hands, he has a lovely wife. Now, *you'd*
know what to do with him. Me, I just shake my head &
take my hat off." I can't guess at how reliably the toad god
zaps the crops with rain—I do know that this faith
in *me* is wholly undeserved. And as for lovely wives... the answer
is: *"Those are the weirdest items tuxedo rental-shops reported
finding in pockets of suits returned to them this year,
a fashion magazine says,"* and with that

thematizing of what had looked like data chaos, she
turns out the light, and fluffles the pillows, and
starts her billowy downslip into sleep. And leaves me
wakeful—leaves me wildly trying to think of pockets adequate
to *everything*: The ashtree staff of the hermit
on his mountaintop for seventeen years. The latest Nintendo
epic, *Callow Drooling Wombat Warriors*. The doctors
cracking open Nicky's sternum like a matzoh—he was five.
The perfect wedge of brie John found one dawn on his car hood.
Gunshots. Twill weft. Owl-hoo. Storm, and calm.
The poem as fit receptacle. Sure. Right.
I'll know what to do with them.

The annual Chutney (& Piccalilli Division) Judging costume ball's
a boffo testosterone/estrus-powered, fanny-wagging hoot.
A western desperado's svelte enamorata's Roman toga-clad.
A Viking gallivants with a Benny-sent-me flapper. Randyness
would seem to be the matrix in which otherwise sequential
ages of humankind dance to the rousing sound of "The Chowchows"
simultaneously. So: Betsy Ross and Genghis Khan are couple
number one in the lambada competition. Nero fiddles while
Joan of Arc burns. It's a giddy vision, but ultimately
persuasive of the way life truly functions: as a simulcast,

that works in modest circumstance as well. In
Lucas Cranach's *Samson and Delilah*, that title twosome
is resplendently dressed in the lady-and-courtier finery
familiar to Cranach's own sixteenth-century German imagination
—he *was* Court Painter to the Electors of Saxony (Wittenberg).
The castle in the background. The light-picked detailwork
on Samson's greaves. The medievally-armored soldiers.
And Delilah is busy weakening him with a most
post-Biblical pair of delicate sewing-basket scissors!
Not only his seemly dove-brown hair, then, but the fabric

of chronology itself is being undone as we watch. Or
friends of mine in bed: he wakes and, after seven years
of marriage, sees her through the ghost-slick of an earlier lover
—endless tiny this-and-that comparisons of flesh and style.
Then he sleeps, *she* wakes: and takes a similar long
half-fond, half-pitiless look at *him* in time-montage...
Our *now* is always broken by the rising of the living past,
the way in 1938 that trawler netted up a live coelacanth
("extinct" since the Devonian), fierce and bony.
"All ages are contemporaneous," saith Pound,

"in the mind"—which is the lesson of the uterus, too:
that what we were is what we are, compounded and
neocortically charged; but the beast, and before it
the germinant ocean flesh, is always with us.
Or anyway, that's what it seems like here; an astronaut
unhelmets himself and with his teeth unlaces the willing
bodice of a stout Shakespearian tavern wench.... And so
we seek each other out, samurai and Nefertiti,
suffragette and Elvis clone—partners, in the knowledge that
the taste between the legs is news from home.

ACROSS TOWN

For the rest of the day, the lover lifts his fingers
to his nostrils and smells her.

Here he is in The Corner Cafe. Her pungency
becomes the redolent steam of his split-pea soup.

Outside: traffic, bleared by the window.
It's winter and the snow is like a second city on top of the city.

It's winter and ice makes walking a dangerous dance.
And even so, the *shul* is filled with old men come to pray.

The Torah gets paraded and they touch it
with their prayershawl fringe, then kiss the fringe.

I've seen them do it: lifting the fringe to their lips,
like bits of bread soaked through with the Glory.

DOLPHIN IN A ZOOT SUIT
a poem with loose ends

She arrives from Denver—is, she learns, a *colorado*
(strictly speaking, *-da*) herself: a redhead. "Welcome,
señorita, to the land of fish-in-the-trees." To reach this
funkily jungley, river-tangled pocket of Peru,
she's been in serial vehicle devolution for three days,
from the snappily professional care of a stewardess
(with a beverage cart that glittered like some secret Vatican treasure),
through a sleeking city taxi, then a lowlands village taxi
hacking oilglop and held together by *chicle*, and now
to a daylong trip up the dawdling and chocolatey river
in a *peque-peque*, a seemingly toy-like engine atop
a dugout canoe. She hugs her luggage and camcorder case
like shields: or else she'll also unevolve. And
it's true: in "raintime," river water rises 30 feet, and *bufeo*

colorado—the area's little-studied but legendary "pink dolphin,"
not an ocean but truly a *river* dolphin—neatly loops about
these trees at a height that formerly sheltered tufted monkeys,
snortles after its food or side-rolls in the easy play
of a picnicker lazying over the ruins of buried Roman causeways.
Eight feet long. As much as 340 pounds. Its comic, tubular,
almost proboscissy shnozz admits ten pounds of fish a day.
The *colorado:* a flush of rosé in its skin. *Her*
colorado: her story, her cover piece for *Nature Talk*,
her longed-for break in the ecoreporter biz. But
this is no afternoon of butterfly nets in a meadow. A month
of living in the open-sided A-frames that they grandly call
the Ranger Post, of bathing out of buckets, and
of shaking angry greensnakes from the bedroll, looms
impossibly; and as for the loutish "rangers"...crimiNEE! Maxímo

swats a ten-inch venomous spider roughly off her back
as she's asleep; good, sure; but what was he doing there
watching her, huh? *His* soles are calloused into human
hooves; *she* slices open *her* toe on a stone at the turtle-egg hatchery
and it festers, gummy. Jorge grunts and farts and
tends the tank of arawana fish as if they're living slivers
of himself, he's so surprisingly gentle. Hours steam away
in heat and ennui, and then something unexpectedly raw and
glorious will happen—when a shock of macaws flaps on high
(*so* bright!) it looks like a scatter of Little Golden Books
in flight. Maxímo salves her toe, the full foot, both feet.
Writing. Camera work. Revising. It isn't surprising,
is it?—in the greenblack pit of the night, one night
a week before she leaves, she takes Maxímo for a lover

in this poem, in the flowing of artifice-time:
it's all we know of them really. But life is messier
than its depiction, of course; life, and the bottomless psyche.
So the stewardess, whom we perceive as a function
of being "the stewardess," in a thinly linear construct:
do we *want* to know about the year in law school
lousied-up by partyheartyfests with Theo-poo,
the high-camp drag drugmeister; yes, we do; and
no, the circuitry of our own nights is already overloaded.
We could open her like the screen of a CD-ROM and mouse away
inside, accessing, zooming in, forever; her, or Roe
the harried impresario of the *Taxi Fantastico* one-car fleet,
but... no thanks. It's enough for me to try to sketch this scene:
our rendezvousers "share mosquito netting" (idiomatic

locally for "sleep together") that night and all seven nights
that week (or sometimes "set the net on fire").

Work continues, though. Maxímo deftly swishes his canoe
amid the sandbars, swiftly first and then more sluggishly
entering deeper, broader, tannin-colored water: it's
so thickly brown, the dolphins sporting finger-length below
the side of a prow are only bubble-trails. *They,* however,
have echo-location and sensory hairs in their meaty beaks,
and zero-in on their prey in an undulant snap. Maxímo
has seen up to 35 of them, finely-tuned as a unit,
herding and banking their fish. That's what he's doing today:
a "fin count." What *she's* doing is watching what *he's* doing,
writing it: entering the deeper, broader language. "Tell me
more about them." *Listen then.* He tells her

a story: *The grandmothers say: in Iquitos they say:*
at the dance one night, the comeliest girl in the village,
we'll call her Horténsia, strayed out to see those enormous
butterfat stars they have there popping in the sky, and she met
a redhead dandy waiting at the riverbank, he
was wearing a linen suit as white as the hanky
the generalissimo's mistress waves at the parade, he
had a honnerdollar Panama hat and a gold watch on a chain,
oh he was smoooooth, and they made perfect love
right there on the slick of the bank (he kept his hat on), hey
if they had *had any mosquito netting: ssst, in ashes!*
But afterwards, playing, she grabbed his hat—and so she saw
the blowhole. And he ran and dived in the water, so smooooooth
it accepted him back home without a ripple

—is a story of how everybody has another self;
say, a reverse-self. And as if to underscore—or, more,
*sub*underscore—this notion with a word from the world
of funded *nuevo*-physics research, the U of Paris
Waves and Acoustics Laboratory is busy perfecting
a "time-reversal mirror" of piezoelectric ceramic slivers: it
bounces an echo back exactly backwards (many medical
and industrial applications, they avow)—the kind of thing she'd know
from the in-fax stack at *Nature Talk,* and knows *here* too,
in the language of here: At night, the river becomes a still and black
reflective surface—in effect, becomes the sky, and holds
the sky's own stippled fire; while overhead, the nexused stars
ribernos call "The Dolphin" leap majestically,
a great arc through the universe's currents. She

feels some nights, in the bug-buzz lulls, as if she's also
yanked by unseen powers inside-out, and that some inner lining,
viney and crawley and ova-filled—a second capability
of Denver-her amid the malls and the infocasts—emerges here,
invincible and panting. Everyone, tonight, is silent: introspective.
Jorge studying up on salt solutions. Manuel lost
in cable repair—she thinks of it as "manuel labor." Maxímo engrossed,
inventing a heating coil for the sand at the turtle hatchery
and thinking, thinking… gazillions of miles away he has a wife
he left, Horténsia. He ruined their life
to learn to save the lives of river dolphins. Is it
worth it? He's fashioned a perfect coil, an absolutely lovely
and functional perfect heating coil; and made so much
emotional wreckage. Who *is* he anyway, he asks the night

as if the night has never heard this philosophical caterwaul
in all of its post-Big-Bangian days, as if the sky has never once
read over the shoulder of someone composing an anomie-steeped
    poem
in a bedside journal. Ah, the night sky knows: it's everywhere,
the celebrated moon appears, and then so does the wolf-,
and so does the leopard-, and so does the pluméd serpent-, in-us.
Who *are* we? What smidgeon of antimatter-us
do we necessarily bear? "In 1988, in the journal *Psychological Medicine*,
a group of psychiatrists told of their own cases
of lycanthropy. Their narratives include two Cats,
two Wolves, a Dog, a Bird, a Rabbit, a Gerbil,
and two 'Unspeakables.'" For one folk, it's a lion: someone
is beat; is cruelly beat; the way milk can be beat
—until something golden is formed. Another story

reverses the roles, but remains the same story: *Once*
(they say) this big-boned farm boy down from the plateau
to meet a sweetheart for the night was stopped
tongue-out in his tracks at the sight of a redhead dazzler
wriggling her hips like jazz and spilling from the slits
in a hot pink slither-hither gown. And she said if
only he'd wear this blindfold that she had, she'd diddle
him twice around the world. He did, she did,
the clay they lay on at the river's edge was almost heated
enough to turn ceramic. Oh but when they finished he
peeked. Her wig had slipped. And so he saw
where he'd been doing it. As he gasped, she fell
like water into the water, and left him staring
at the otherworld dew all over his cock. These creatures

inspire just such fired-up fancies: that they speak to us
in dreams, that they're the gods of the river, etc.
But lolling along the shore to watch their actual habits is
the better wonder. Witnessing the dorsal ridge of an antic calf
that's scoring tiny flourishes around its mother's swim:
is a sufficient day. To lean against the white bark
of a cecropia trunk, a little drunk on the nearly acrylic
vivacity of the toucans: a sufficient day. Or almost. It's
her last day here—the itch of home is on her.
A dolphin, by being a dolphin, *is* doing its job
in the web of interconnections; her job's elsewhere though, and
(looking at him fossicking over the heating coil) elsewhom. Denver
calls. We find her moping, torn; we leave her—in this poem of loose
ends—suffering the richness of the cosmos, that we humans feel

only as distraction and impingement. She'll receive an award
for her story. The rivers will ebb, will slowly choke with silt,
will rise again in time. A man will wake and find a wispy brick-red
tangle of her hair on his mat, and walk to the water's edge
and gently set it like a child's paper boat on the current,
and watch it sail out into a herd of "pinks" that bask
so thickly in the river it looks cobbled. No: he's
stormier than that, and it's his labored-over coil
that he pitches in a fit of ire-at-everything
into the hurrying flow. Some people work to save
entire species from extinction, yet can't keep
their own ongoing lives intact. It's night. In the light
of the hurricane lamp he thinks: *Her plane*
disappears in the sky as if it's dived inside blue water.

THE TWO DOMAINS

in several voices

overture

A heavy, violent sky:
ironmongery and smithy forges.
A night for murder. Then it settles
out of its kettledrum drama,
into zitherstrings of drizzle,
into a morning of drizzle, a noon
of after-drizzle, and a dusk of thick long fog.
A day for ghosts.
The year is 1888. The subject is
Samuel and Liza Ruby Williams,
dead on their honeymoon night
of random rifle-fire from a feud they aren't part of,
in a gabled hotel near the seacoast shingle.
That's all we know. The rest is fog,
is salt air eating up details.
Generations pass. It's now,
we're here. Hello.
A poem is about to begin. The sun
appears above the horizon, limited at first, like someone
matter-of-factly entering a warehouse, with a flashlight.
Then the overheads get turned on.
Time to start. The sun is taking its daily
inventory, shining with impartial force on every row
of what we know
and what we don't know.

✳

We don't *know* if the Yeti really
stomps its great splayed cinquefoil prints
up icy goat-paths at the Top of the World, though
there are over seven decades of photographs,
and spoor, and depositions
taken somberly with the breaths of the testifiers
afloat like lovely, ivory jellyfish in the Himalayan air.
Yeti. Sasquatch. Nessie. The Surrey Puma.
The thirty-foot Tatzelwurm of the Alps.
Iffy fellow creatures of an ecosphere beyond
Linnaean tagging. We don't know what improbable
vehicle spun like a pinwheel for Ezekiel,
or didn't, in the desert's shimmervision,
we don't know if the boggling monologues that so
stirred Joan of Arc were in- or exterior, or
what transcendent gizmo (or quintessence) (or infinitessence)
    speaking
at the heart of the Bush on the Mountain—what
Rosetta Fire—deciphered the thought of the Lord Almighty
into the language of wandering tribesmen. We don't know.
Kaspar Hauser: who? Amelia Earhart: where?
The Shroud of Turin: how? and even: what?
The sky folds open over the otherwise unremarkable
village of Cam-at-Wye, and a minutes-long fall
of ibises and cormorants—hundreds, dead but spookily perfect,
as if killed by a look, and then preserved in salt—
heaps up the gutters and thunks on top
of the fish-and-chips carts. O we never tire of this
unending catalogue of what-we-don't-know,
of Tut and Bigfoot and Jack the Ripper: maybe they
distract us from more intimate not-knowings. There are strange
    beasts
at the back of every brain, and there is burning inside every heart
but, lo! the heart is not consumed, the heart is not consumed

but burns with want and fear unceasingly, and
why we're who we are, and how to get through any day of it,
we don't know—so,
"I have seen the tracks of mountain bears on numerous occasions.
Believe me: *these* are not tracks of a bear in snow."

"You dirty-mind SON-OF-A-BITCH!"
(the splat of a flung ceramic saucer)
(a slap: the flat of a hand to a cheek)
"Yeah? THAT'S for calling names..."
(once more: a smack)
"...and THAT'S to give to your weirdo freak of a son,
who stole my lapel pin today, and when I catch him
I'm going to kayo his ass from here to TimbucTOO."
"He took your pin? No."
"Yes, I sez."
"Oh, bay-*bee*... I'm sorry."
(some rustling sounds: then very damp moaning, very low)
(tiptoe noise over linoleum: the boy slips out the back porch door)

*

My profession, my job, my—I would say
my calling. And this is why: there was a nowhere-land
of uncompleted viaducts and abandoned drainage pipes
a child could hide in, could be lost in, that, when I was a child,
dour adult wisdom determined off-limits, and
to which I ran to hide in with limitless dedication anyway,
day after day. When I was… seven or so, eight. I was
a troubled seven or eight, in that troubled-up house
with her shifty series of live-in pseudo-husbands ("uncle" X,
Y, Z): "Hey, you spell trouble, buster," she'd always observe,
and I came to learn this meant—but of course—he'd be staying
a season or two, until her ire started powering
kitchen dishes through the air again ("I'm WARNing you,
lady" / *duck* / SMASH) with a rapid flight of saucer
after saucer, of the kind (for this was 1955)
the UFO believers watched for, on a larger level. I
was a fey and elfin thing, in the midst of this
melmac-and-pinkyring opera. And the more
I fumbled mumbletypeg and petty theft and spudball—all
of the standard boyhood pastimes in my neighborhood—the more
I was alone, and longed to be alone, and had predictive
dreams (that cat we found half-dead from hunger on the stoop,
for one, and also the fire at Zelman's Discount Sundries); and shivered,
or flew inside of myself, in what my mother described as
one of my "moods," or sometimes one of my "witch moods"; and,
defiantly, I'd visit that prohibited nowhere-land
of mazed industrial dead-ends, which was as good
as the Foreign Legion for me, or being lifted mystically to Mars.
Oh I'd *always* heard voices; but those,
they weren't words and didn't have
originating faces. They were insect-music,
planet-music, something inhuman. But then one night,
one runaway night in the pipes, I heard somebody
call my name—from out of my pocket. Inside

I had a garish, chunky, rhinestone men's lapel pin
that I'd play with, for a crystal ball. I took it out.
The air inside the pipes seemed alive—it brushed
my cheeks like a risen nap. It seemed
the microorganism life of the muck was demanding
my child-attention. And my name
came out of the bauble. Someone called my name
—my father called my name, my father
I'd never seen, who was dead, they told me,
before I was born, he called my name
a number of times in a voice I thought of then, and
still can't improve upon, as milky. All night
I hid there, hearing the one word
that was me, intoned repeatedly, with a constance
only the dead know. Then the sun
appeared above the horizon, limited at first, like someone
matter-of-factly entering a warehouse, with a flashlight;
and I headed home, to face
the punitive music. That
was the first time. Now
it's thirty years, and many voices, later. The media
cheapens what I do—they say
"ghostbusters," as if this were an arcade game, or
the rotorootering-out of spectral blockage.
But houses are… troubled,
let's say. Let's say all houses are troubled in ways,
and some in ways its people find
requiring of my talents.
They try others first, I know.
And then they dial my number.
Let's say I'm called.

✳

But we *do* know, assuredly, SLIPCOVER TOP
TURNS ANY BROOM INTO A MOP! (its "Fleecy Head Grabs
  Dirt!")
and EASY-STRIPPER ZIPS OFF PAINT
WITHOUT STRENUOUS SANDING, SCRAPING, OR DANGER-
  OUS CHEMICALS,
fourteen-ninety-eight. The age of the fishes and loaves,
of the pillar of cloud and the pillar of fire, is long, long gone,
and a day is an irksome, crummy thing, but still we know that
in our darkest hour
MIRACLE KLEEN and MAGIC SPONGE and MIRACLE CAR
  BRUSH work "in a snap!" and that their snazzy confrere,
MR. WASHABLE, REUSABLE LINT-OFF ROLLER, consists
of "Space Age Material"—"Great…" (if that's not
understating it) "…Stocking Stuffer!" Yes! And
SUPERKEGEL HELPS END INCONTINENCE and
AUTOMATIC CARD DECK SHUFFLER is "Great for Arthritics,"
and CORDLESS ELECTRIC SAFETY TRIMMER
NEATLY REMOVES UNSIGHTLY NOSE, EAR, BROW HAIR
QUICKLY, PAINLESSLY, with the merest of swiveled insertions.
We *know* this. It uses one double-A battery, and fits in purse
or glove compartment, and comes in vinyl carrying sheath,
and if it tumbled from out of the heavens
onto the ziggurat-dotted Babylonian plains, the peoples
there and then would build it a golden altar of wingéd bulls
and never again let it touch the defiling ground.
A day is a burdensome thing. A day is an entropic, burdensome thing,
and moves to the random piping of Chaos,
a multigalactic organization represented on Earth by the firm
of Mess and Clutter. But still we know that
OVERSIZED FOLDING LAUNDRY RACK OFFERS OVER
79 FEET OF DRYING SPACE, and here to help
in that valiant effort are SLIDING UNDER-SINK ORGANIZER
and TILT-FRONT WICKER HAMPER and UNDER-BED

STORAGE BOX and COMMUTER SHOE TOTE and
OVER-SINK SHELF and DISPENSE-A-BAG, o *everything*
is accounted for, and CEDAR TOOTHPICK TOTE
"Keeps Toothpicks Always Handy and Sanitary Too!"
The sky is endless, the world of particle and wave by definition
is unknowable, the sky will swallow the grandest plan
and shit it out ulcered in fungus. Still, we
lattice the sky with recognizable pattern, Cup, Bear, Throne.
And so we rung a day, we give ourselves
these handholds to climb through a day, and
I'm happy to say some come in decorator colors,
I'm pleased to announce that polypropylene
"will not rust, dent, or chip," and I'm delighted to know
that I know these things, these sweet dependable things
that are yours, and mine, and come in our sizes,
and are affordable.

✳

"I tell you, that child was no more raised than a weed."

"Oh hush—she'll hear you."

"She's heard worse, I can tell you that. (pause) Gypsies. (pause)
Not *even* a weed, a weed has roots, a place. *She's*
just this patch-together hibbledyjibbledy thing."

"I think—"

"She only knows chaos and mishmash and superstition. It's sinful.
She needs to get a mental... (what's the right word?) ...rolodex."

"I think I hear Mom Bend-your-dick-off coming."

(footsteps)

then (together): "Good evening, Mother Benedicta."

(on the other side of the wall, the girl is suddenly determined: *whatever*
it is, she's going to get herself some rolodex: LOTS of rolodex)

✳

Five years ago, when the business became successful enough—
unmanageable enough, to be frank—and I hired office staff to help me
keep the wayward tufts of the work day neatly tucked, I put up a mod-
est bulletin board at a corner of the corridor, where I told them they
should feel free to express any quibble, compliment or tasteful witti-
cism of their choosing, and next to the bulletin board I fastened a plas-
tic dispenser of 3 x 5 note cards, one of the kind we stock, with the
note cards done as a toilet-paper-like roll of perforated units, with a
small toothed edge for neatly tearing them off, and with a magnetized
pen in a groove along the top. A slow seller, but steady. And I like to
think it's a testimony to how precise I am in choosing office person-
nel, that not one time in all five years has the pen been "missing."

Gretchen, Nora and Ramon are more like family than hired help (I
have no other family, in fact, and if I *had* to have a family, had to select
one in a week, had to interview would-be parents and siblings, I'd try
to model my choices on these three) and the number of complaints
that appear on the bulletin board is close to nil—but a "joke of the
day" is something I always welcome, and some of the puns and jibes
from over the years have later enlivened the catalog.

I may as well say now that I'm the founder and president of a mail-
order company called Notions and More, and I'm proud of the ser-
vice I offer. How shall I put it? Every day, we feel the universe slip out
of our control—friends die, friends stubbornly refuse to follow the
scripts we keep in our heads, impervious marriages suffer erosion and
split asunder, international economies boom or bust along trajecto-
ries of such immense scale they're practically invisible and certainly
beyond our comprehension, the papers are nothing but flood and fire,
fire and flood and savages massing in packs at the city limits, and even-
tually our own bodies begin to betray us.... Well! But the smallest
touches can reassert a sense of organization.

On top of everything else, there shouldn't be the worry over how to launder your baseball cap without its being crumpled in the cycle. (Try my inexpensive ball cap frame, of durable white poly.) Misplaced keys? (My keychain that beeps when you whistle.) "Ring Size Reducers Make Your Rings Fit Properly Without Costly Repairs." (Set of four, only two-ninety-eight.) "Cat Perch Clips Onto Window Sill." "Clear Acrylic Platter With Imbedded White Lace Doily" compliments any table decor, and eliminates need to launder doilies! Suffering, take it from me, has a 24-hour watch set on our houses, but with Ball Cap Door Rack Organizer and Hanging Vinyl Shoe Organizer and Twenty-Compartment Thimble Spinner and Handy Carry-All Tote With Your Name (Up to Fifteen Letters), even Suffering shakes and pales. Do your throw rugs slide? Is your hosiery tangled like orgiastic octopi? These are questions that MIT and Cal-Tech haven't yet tried to answer.

But *I've* stared hard at those questions, unflinching. And tens of thousands of thoroughly satisfied customers (and a few recurrent grumblers) seem to be happy I have—enough so, that next week we expand our operations, adding a humor division (comic slogan t-shirts, underwear, mugs: that kind of thing) and a warehouse section of other businesses' discontinued supplies: a shipment of unused hospital hypodermics, service station funnels, and diner matchbook dispensers, has just come in; I'm waiting now for an order of cocktail shaker sets, some souvenir vials of Holy Water of Lourdes, and turkey-silhouette turkey basters. This branch will be located in a former (rickety, under repair) three-story nineteenth-century hotel, The Golden Gull, a lovely gabled building right near the tide-rippled beach shingle. Ribbon-cutting ceremony is September 1st.

Anyway, *that's* the joke of the day on the bulletin board, from someone: that today I'm expanding and shrinking at the same time. I've been honest with the staff, all three of them know that I've just started seeing a therapist. (Shrinking... maybe for the humor division, "shrink wrap" Christmas gift wrap for your favorite psychotherapist? See if anyone else has done it yet.)

And that's why I'm keeping this journal-of-sorts. Vivian says the small melange of plaints I've brought her way (the "same-ol'- same-ol'" syndrome, she calls it: a thirty-five-year-old's string of tedium) is probably just a matter of six or seven weekly sessions. The journal is her idea, and I'm supposed to report today, at session two, on how it's going. Boringly, I think. (Can I cure tedium by tediously writing? Well, Vivian seems to know her job.)

But I can't write any more now. Ramon was just on the phone, and his voice was... strained. He's been out at The Gull all week, to oversee the stock rooms. "Something's happening here, Miss Carter," he said. "Something's *supposed* to be happening, Ramon: you're fixing up the stock." "No, something bad." "To what degree?" My heart flipflopped. And all he said, in that laconic voice of his, was "Come on out, and bring a broom and a camera and a tape recorder, Miss Carter." So no more journal today.

Hm.

✳

interlude

time: 1888
place: a seacoast hotel / room 8

He: Into this vial I have compressed the vital male principle
from a bullocks, and from a he-bear, and from
the fighting cock that they breed in the hills of the Orient
to wear sharpened malachite spurs. And in this vial
I have collected the female marrow-juice out of the peahen,
and out of the dam-bear, and out of the great
complacent dairy cow of our own well-grazed back pasture,
with her sweet breath and sweet feces. Do you wonder
what I will do now? Do you wonder at this
portable pylon set at the foot of the bed?

She: I do not wonder. Or if I do, I wonder
how cold our dinner is growing in the common-room
at the far end of the hotel. I envy the woman
in the suite above, on her honeymoon, later
tonight *she* will be grazed, yes *she* will be a pasture
open to tongue and teeth, while I curl up here
in these tentacles of sulfur, in the blue sizzle
of your experiments. Why do I do it?
—*that's* what I wonder.

He: I was not speaking to you,
my dearest. I was speaking to Posterity,
and addressing its way
a few academic questions, as transitional devices
in my discourse. Now I must get on
with the Grand Work. As you know, my current scientific equipment
(out of a carpet bag, he begins unpacking
a steady stream of beakers, tubing, electrodes, etc.,

piling it in front of himself)
was acquired with the kindly fiscal enablement
of a gentleman—a speculator in other people's fortunes,
shall we say—who thrice already has sent
his associates my way to request his investment back:
they left a strong and lingering impression
amid the wreckage of our living room, and the sooner
I complete my studies and find the right
appreciator of them, in either government or industry,
the sooner will I be free of those financial bonds,
and the sooner will The Work Itself rise up
like a flame in the midst of our unlit ignorance.
Besides, as you know, it is not becoming…

(she continues moueing into the dressing-table mirror,
arraying before herself an arsenal of cosmetics
and cosmetic dabber-onners,
and a curling iron, wigs, a corset lacing-hook, etc.,
in this way balancing the items of his slapdash laboratory;
as he continues speaking, she intermittently, overlavishly
mouths his words at the mirror)

…for the enamorata of one who has already patented successfully
The Pneumatic Hat-Tipper, The Wonder Suction Restorative,
and The Combination Electric Bedbug Exterminator and
Nighttime Emissions Preventative, it is not becoming,
I tell you, to be so dismissive, even if
charmingly so, my orchid, my bird of paradise.

She: By now they will have completed the ices
and finely diced fruits of the season, and even
the silver tureen of turtle soup will have been returned
to the kitchen, happily emptied; and the presentiment
aroma of a plate of butter-rummed leg of lamb,

with garnee of squash rosettes and a dish of mint jelly,
will be floating above the table in filaments
finer than my hair, which is the finest hair in the county,
as Senator Clamshack has opined, and General Loppingstock.
There will be gaiety at the table, and worldly tales.
But the honeymoon couple will not be there, oh
they will have made their apologies early, retiring
to room 18 above us, there to satisfy
hungers of such a basic and elemental nature,
as to make the startling crackles that I brush through my hair
become a virtual lightning storm, in empathy with their passions.

He: And what of this portable pylon set at the foot of the bed,
you inquire. And I reply: With this,
I will generate fiercesome power through my separate vials
of gender-resplendent ichors, and I will simplify,
and emulsify, and mix, and remix, and render,
until finally I have a single vial
of Salient Human Liquid—the One, the Whole, the perfect marriage
of male and female, so that imbalances of our wholeness
(and *who* knows *how* many common infirmities this covers?)
can be ministered to, with the proper application of this,
my Medicant of the Ages!

She: I wonder if it will cure a case
of rampant garrulosity of the talkus-loquacious,
my dashing, my ram.

He: Oh don't feed *me* your lavenderwatered
nyaah-nyaah-nyaahs of envy and derision!

She: Well—

He: So—

(sudden knocking on the door)

Voice: Your fish dinner is here.

*(she motions him to the door, with the frantic gestures
of the dinner-deprived; he opens it; the rest happens quickly:)*

Voice: COMPLIMENTS OF LOUIE THE FISH!

(blam! blam! blam!)

(screams; running)

✳

We don't *know* if the *ba*,
that elegant hawk-with-a-human-head
(the head of the deceased), *does*
periodically return to the tomb
to hover over its mummy and feed on the funerary offerings,
but the literature attests to this, and also that
"they flutter under the rays of heaven and speak
with words of weeping," and also that other possible shapes
"are as a heron or swallow, a falcon or bittern,
whichever thou pleasest" (the hawk, though, is the hieroglyph);
on a mummycase now in Copenhagen, the carven *ba*
is at the side of its carven mummy with sad familiarity
that makes it seem as if it would mew
instead of skreel a raptor's cry, and the *ba* shown
on the Papyrus of Ani seems to be leisurely sculling
through the thick, closed air of the tomb, its wings like oars
that have been draped in beautiful feather-pattern afghans.
Birds—as one example. So seemingly easy and everyday
a thing as birds—and we don't know. The rukh,
or roc, of Marco Polo and Sindbad: "one of them
can pounce upon an elephant and bear it aloft."
The gryphon. The phoenix. Whatever "real" bird is their
explanatory provenance. We don't know. (In February
1992, a golden eagle "plucked a day-old lamb from a field"
near Chinnor, in Buckinghamshire, "and killed it nearby.")
Since 1880, New Zealand has given rise to nine alleged
sudden sightings of a moa—that wingless, ostrich-more-or-lessish,
six-foot-tall bird, thought to be extinct
by 500 years. Who knows? A new species of bird
was first reported in October 1992 (New Guinea's
hooded pitohui, whose feathers and flesh are naturally
saturated with powerful poison, "10 milligrams of which
is enough to kill a mouse or frog")—so who knows?
The rain of bird blood (so claimed by the Italian

Meteorological Bureau) in May 1890. The Holy Ghost
as dove. The Thunderbird. What do we know, and how lightly
does it fly from our fingers? Of Tut's tomb, even
seven decades after its excavation: "It is impossible
to determine the original position of…" and "Nor
does one know where…" etc. Now does he hunt
the Nile duck and the succulent river goose
in the reeds of the Afterlife? We don't know,
and it flocks in the air. We don't know, and it
filleth the skies with its mocking keen,
it darkens the land, the way the swarming
wild passenger pigeon did for Audubon,
"until we were benighted by that solid overhead mass."

*

The invisible, ectoplasmic stitch by which
the worlds attach—I mean this world
of human interplay and baskets of radish
and airport paperback spinner racks; and
the other world, of otherbeings
living out the terms of other spatialness—
is a perilous place to be, if "be"
is even vaguely accurate, if modes of concentration
can be places. You see?—I only have the language
of the world of human interplay, and it is,
I'm sorry, insufficient. Let me try this:
when a friend of mine goes bow-hunting deer,
he wears the colors "tree," and clambers into a tree
where he waits all day, unmoving and scented
in deer pee. Me?—I
"ghostify" myself, I go a partum-epidermis closer
to *that* world. It isn't a visible change
(although I might start in a trance), I'm not
translucent in a moment. I don't begin
to fume like a block of dry ice. But
mentally I *do* flimmer a receptivity—a willingness—
toward the plane of ghostly presences
(I think of it as "the twixtworld") and I don't exist
right then so much as *transist*.
Sometimes nothing happens. I grope my way
like a mole's starred snout
through empty psychic goop, and
nothing happens. There are other times...
they come, with their various grievances and signs.
And we start talking.

*   *   *

In *Landscape in the Style of Ni Tsan*
by Wang Yu (dated 1690), the fisherman/scholar
seems to glide in his sketchy one-man craft
on breath, from out of breath, and into an endlessness
of breath, like a gnat
into billows of stiffened eggwhite—no,
the eggwhite has more substance, more
interior geography, than this
suffusion of mist-and-void
we lose ourselves in, looking. I'd go
ghostified that way, into the spectral realm,
and sometimes *so* successfully
be a part of its acorporealness,
the way back wavered like smoke, and started
blowing away like smoke, past
my reclaiming. I was always bad
at the things of *our* world: income tax
has left my mind as well as my desktop
something like the rubble after a bombing raid,
and studying the absolutely untranslatable
zeppelin rudders and robots' bungs and metal lasagna
under my car hood leaves me
ineffectually giggling—I'm up-front about this
with clients—but set me to parley with a wandering spirit,
and I can cross the border
speaking spiritese in a jiffy. There have been times
when only the serendipitous squeal of outside traffic,
or a jackhammer's clamor, or baby's squawl
—some tendril of Earthly interconnection suddenly
beseeching—served to rouse me, and bring me
hand-over-hand up its length, back
to the body.

*   *   *

In that, I'm somewhat like a ghost.
They have a tendril yet
that ties them to the world of the living.
The tendril's the problem.
There's no such thing as a ghost without a problem,
a ghost without a request.
You can't tell from the photographs.
Under that sepia administered like a ham glaze,
everyone's uniformly grim
or uniformly pitching smiles at the camera like softballs.
Some, though, will die
with a quiet acceptance, wanly waving
one last time,
as if for the nailpolish to dry.
While some... the air
inside the air is torn, is stained, with the violent, struggling
reluctance of their going. Maybe a vow
is unfulfilled, maybe a love is sundered, it could be
even a hate is sundered—a tendril,
an anchor, that keeps them from becoming
elementary again. And all I do
—it's usually simple—is help them snap
that tie. I once delivered up
the cloth bag of a stillbirth buried for twenty-nine years
behind the back porch steps,
so someone dead for twenty-seven years
could offer a humble prayer of goodbye
that she'd been too ashamed to make at the time.

*   *   *

This case. This wonderful case! You know
the clanking chains, the creaking stair, the clouded mirror.
Last week I was called to a warehouse:
hundreds of mirrors, ladies'-purse-sized compact mirrors,
flying through the air like jet maneuvers on the Fourth,

then crashing like supersonic kamikaze lemmings into a wall!
Ten gross of plastic parrots (purple and yellow residua
from some out-of-business cake-top decoration company)
swooooping through the room, and making this chowdery seacoast
  building
(an abandoned hotel) the tropics! Of course,
as is typical, I followed the police,
five university professors from geology and physics,
a priest, and—obviously—the media, though
my client seems proficient in keeping those video vultures
mollified and away. Weeks passed.
The factory-reject hi-ball glasses continued to soar and dive.
So now it's my turn. It isn't that these
specific spirits are any more troubled than most
—but what fine props they've been given! Ah, but
my client! She's driving me crazier than nosediving rosebud vases
ever could. I need to sign in. I need to sign out.
I need to file receipts each day in some elaborate
color-coded accordion-like case with a microchip lock.
She doesn't believe in what I'm doing, and she *tells* me
she doesn't believe in what I'm doing, even while telling me
how to most efficiently do it
(using her Sleep-Eze White Noise Hum Machine for trance states
was her yesterday's suggestion). After an hour
of her overlyorderly fussing, I finally
ghostified myself... the world turned fog
so thick I could grab it like bolls of cotton...
there were shapes in the fog... the first
faint feeling of contact... and
her fucking beeper watch sounded.
I told her: it only takes one pinhole
in the darkroom wall to ruin things—right?
I told her *she* was liable to be one
more ghost here before the day was out.

On the way home, in a deserted stretch
of rocky coast, with rain coming on,
the car died. And after my panic attack,
I did, I admit, take out the pamphlet
she'd pressed on me insistingly this morning,
Car Survival Step By Step, and in the pitiful flicker
of light remaining, I did plug wire one
to wire two, and the car did start again,
I admit it. And now I also own the voluminous pleasures
of *Income Tax From A to Z.*

✳

But we *do* know the feather is keratin.
A bird about the size of a swan has twentyfive-thousand-*million*
barbule filaments in a single feather. The hummingbird
beats its wings as fast as eighty times a second, so hovers
over its chosen blossom inside brilliant
ruby-and-emerald parentheses of its own making. The beak
of the Andean sword-billed hummingbird is four times
the length of its body: a nectar-sucker. The beak
of the buzzard wouldn't be out of place on a tool-shed wall.
We know this. The beak is keratin as well, and we know
its kajillion manifestations, tong-beaks, skimmers, drills,
the intricate sieve-and-pump beak of the flamingo,
the robin's forthright pinch. We know these sketched
and graphed and (lately) computer-enhanced or video'd things, these
fascinating, indexed things, these bounteous, *countless*
ornithological wonderments-turned-facts. The cassowary
is a loner; twenty-thousand pairs of gannets
will nest in a colony that looks like a swatch
of French petit point. Jackdaws, starlings and jays
are known to pick up individual ants in their beaks
—a kind of ant that spouts out formic acid—and
swab their bodies with these: a way of killing
fleas and lice originally, but sometimes now become
a form a pleasure, so that they also "ant" their bodies
for excitement with wasps, with pebble-edges, even
lit cigarette ends. The sooty tern will fly
for up to four years without landing. Some birds:
ruffled pompadours. Cheerleader pompoms. Fluffed-up
barroom darts. Three geese will make a sexual
ménage-à-trois. A cardinal will feed a gaping
goldfish, so alike is the visual stimulus. We
know this, and know more than this, we trove it away, then
go out and look to know more. We've always been looking:
Keats's nightingale; Shelley's skylark; the stalwart, heraldic

herring gull of a sketchbook *circa* 1400. In fact,
our info list on the gull alone is encyclopedias'-worth.
The semiotics of body posture (the herring gull
from 1400 is, presumably, captured in the "upright stance
of intended aggression"). The research on which of many possible signals
induces a herring gull chick to beg food from its parent
(it's the red spot on the parent-bird's bright yellow lower mandible).
The nesting patterns of kittiwake gulls. The survival value
of camouflaged eggs. The "courtship feed" (the cock-gull
vomiting fish or offal onto the ground in front of the hen, or
—this among kittiwakes—into her opened gullet).
Birds in literature (The Golden Gull). Or birds in aerodynamics studies.
The folklore of birds. The jazzman: "Bird." The birds of major sports
    teams.
Knowledge. Treatises: emu, cockatoo, quail. So much
we know, so much we need
to know: to salt its tail.

✳

September 28

Flustered. Flummoxed. Frantic. Panicked. I've always been one to check *Roget's*, I *like* going down its orderly rows, like walking a well-tended garden and sampling the flowerings there. But no word even comes close.

The ribbon-cutting ceremony has been, of course, delayed. The loan from the Northeast Business Association has been consigned to a fiscal limbo. Ramon has quit—an insubordination I *will not* tolerate. But who can blame him? Yesterday a flock of plastic spatulas zoomed through the room.

I'm almost used to it by now. It has an eerie grace. It's come to be predictable—the ghastly moans, the circumnavigation of the goblets—I can live with something predictable.

But this moonstruck, clutter-skulled, gamin-eyed ghost exterminator that Nora finally persuaded me to hire...! Grrr.

When I was a child, back in the Home, I came to admire—maybe I can even say I came to love—the thrice-a-day methodical call to prayer of the bells. They made / how can I say this? Although it was invisible, they made a *structure* I could depend on. They turned time into an architecture.

But what I couldn't bear (and couldn't say I couldn't bear, not then, not there) was the moopy, goopy content of the services themselves. There's only so much fluttery talk of fluttery Spirit a person can take.

He's spent all week with his eyes rolled up, like hardboiled eggs in his head. His "initial approach."

He doesn't wear a watch. *I've hired someone who doesn't wear a watch.*

As current recording secretary of Business Card Collectors International, I'm supposed to have had the August minutes transcribed by now, and available to the membership. Beyond that, I had promised to research a handier way of arranging cards for display—it's exactly the kind of practical challenge I enjoy. But of course that hasn't happened. *Nothing* has happened, except for "tangle-free" pocket combs and shotglasses banking off walls.

Samantha, the lawyer's assistant, called. She doesn't think I can sue the company that sold me the damn hotel. There are, she drily said, some things a termite inspection will not cover.

He's lighting black candles today. Mr. Mood. Mr. Cloud. Mr. Haunted House.

*   *   *

The original hotel sign, which I've tastefully restored and kept in front, is a wooden shingle with its eponymous (*Roget* there) golden gull done in a charmingly clunky folk art way: and I reproduced it, flying into the sun, for my business's logo, only stylized—*moderne,* as Gretchen says with a prideful hoity-toity Gallic gurgle. It's on my new business cards.

Ten thousand business cards.

He's standing out in the rain right now, poor thing, in mismatched tennis shoes.

*   *   *

I brought him one of my Pocket Rain Ponchos. He growled. I guess I interrupted some séancely palaver with the infinite, silly me. Mr. Pneumonia. Whatever it was, it seemed to be ruined, and so we drove to lunch through a sulky drizzle. He told me still more stories about the spirit world, early mediums who hoaxed the public, Houdini.

He's into his "second approach," and says a solution should only be a day or two away. Then no more pencil sharpeners doing the watusi, he said. It must have been the first time I've laughed in a month. What a martini will do.

Miss Ruler Edge. Mr. Ouija Words.

*   *   *

Why am I even writing these things, keeping this journal? I never made my second visit to Vivian's therapeutic couch.

I said to Nora: I'm too busy.

And yesterday Nora said to me: It's amazing, I'd think that lately you'd be even *more* flipped-out than you were before, you know, more tense, and more shrink-needy. But if anything, you're *calmer*.

Well, if my problem really *was* tedium...

Then I don't have a problem *now,* do I?

*   *   *

He brought champagne tonight, and we had a "ghost toast." He says he believes we're ready.

I actually think I'll miss those migrating ballpoint pens and faux bone buttons.

October 2

Something happened tonight.

I mean

More later.

*

interlude

time: 1888
place: a seacoast hotel / room 18

He: I'm a simple man,
I'm a steak-and-potatoes man.
My brother Silas and your sister's husband Dell
have kindly sponsored this honeymoon night
at a hotel that pretends to a kind of homespun
ritziness, and I appreciate this generous sign
of their blessing our union, but even so
I'm not a man for terrapin nor the mango chutney
that quivered on its white plate
like the pudding-meats of a squirrel
when I first chuck it into the gutting bag; and
so we've made our excuses and returned
to our room before the third course, and lit
the candles you brought, that are scented of fennel.

She: Is that why we left the dinner table?
Really (*shyly*) is that why we left the dinner table?

He: No. I'm so simple a man,
I'm still a boy. I'm a steak-and-potatoes boy...

She: I love that in you.

He: ...and I didn't know how to say it,
but I say it now, and to your face
that opens and closes and opens again in the candlelight
with the complicated shadows of a rose or a lettuce:
we've come back to the room because we couldn't wait
another slurp of prawn-and-pumpkin-consomme longer

to consummate our love!
(falls to his knees before her)
I haven't wept since I was ten, and Festus died.
I placed my lucky penny inside his jaws
and we buried him out near the wild columbine.

She: I'm weeping too! The candlelight
licking the corners of the room, the heirloom double-ring quilt
that my Aunt Teodora gave us and that I packed
in the leather satchel below a layer of lilac sachet,
your own enormous passion I can see is exploding
deep inside you like fireworks bursting forth in a foreign country...
everything is alive with an animal beauty!
I'm so glad we waited. Even when your tongue discovered
a nerve at the base of my neck that made me feel
as if my body stretched to the moon and back
and contained the heaving Atlantic, even then
we waited, my agitated muscles-flexing boy/man
kneeling before me in your brand-new nankeen trousers and suspenders
(and only that), and I in my sleeping gown
with the delicate shell-pink ribbon trim (and only that)
——this is what we have waited for.

He: Oh I wish at this moment
I had the gift of golden-tongued expression,
like that wild-eyed Professor in the room below,
who we met yesterday in the whist room,
and whose speechifying left the ladies
intoxicated on language—*then*
I would come to you with the proper words of endearment,
lust, and fidelity.

She: You ninny. That Professor
is a gassy fossil. And, as you know, your tongue may not be gold,

but it can mine
my treasures exquisitely. Come
(she opens her arms)
the stars are sprinkled across the night
like the angels' own bijoux, and this is our hour,
and this is its first impetuous minute.
Come—

(noises)

He: There's some commotion below in the corridor.

She: Let's peek out and see.

(They open the door an inch, peer out. More noises, shouting. They look at each other questioningly, and they both step gingerly into the hall:)

(some seconds of silence; then:

blam! blam! blam!)

✳

We don't *know* what's truly shakin' in the basement clubs
of matter: we don't know what sax,
what open, throaty, come-an'-get-it laugh,
what tinkle of change on the bar, is filling
the joss-sweet air there in the back rooms
of the protons and electrons in a rock or a Chinese elm
or the hand on your hip as you sleep.
We look, but we don't know. The very looking
alters the rules of the game as often, as continuously,
as the look itself occurs. That sassy,
flash-and-zen atonal trio,
Quark and Quasar and "Doctor" Quantum Physics,
sways in waves on the stage,
in a slick of sweat so seemingly sublime
that they can tickle tunes out of the vacuum
in the pulse of the heart of antimatter: all night
bringing the house to its feet
or its knees with their stable of favorites,
Probability Theory Blues and *As I Wandered the Streets*
of the Black Hole and *Electroweak Baby o' Mine*,
and the rest; but *we* can't hear these viably enough,
and what do these have to do
with the price of a can of beans, although
this building block *amour* and *triste* and cello dub-dub-dub
is taking place in the tin, and the beans,
and the price, and the living and dying eyes of the girl
who rings it up at the counter. Dub-dub-dub,
and wah-wah-wah, and at the dance floor everybody circles
their favorite rhythmbellied couples,
Death and Transcendence, Being and Non-Being, and
(the surefire winner) Sex and Divinity, as they slither-step
in the dark of Le Club Impossible, and the bubbles of *-on*
float giddily through the air: I mean boson,
fermion, lepton, gravitron, gluon, baryon, hadron, muon,

and the most evanescent, keep-on through another crap day.
We'll never find that winding, unlit street,
although we've been given a map. We'll never get past
the front door. But one note of that music,
the size of a paramecium, is always swimming crazily
up the vein that snakes at the side of an ear, at the temple,
and sends us correspondingly crazy
with brainsick longing. And we'll never exit
the club's back door, to the alley, to open the trashcan there,
and dig through the gristle,
the tripe, the kraut, the spit-up bones,
and wrestle out
the bottommost rag-wrapped shoebox,
sloppily crusted in old yolk blackened to coal, and
finally face the no-face of the secret
our languages all call—when their other words sicken
and fail—the soul.

✳

Once, the great Sasha Mangini negotiated the vanishing
of the persistent after-images of a family of seven
circus aerialists, who had died as one
in a big top fire and stayed, like the odor of smoke
in a pillow, to haunt the grounds for years.
Once, Alma Lorttimer—although very few
were destined ever to know it—rid
the White House itself (I won't say during
whose term) of a baleful presence that moved
among the gilded furniture and portraits
like a smudgepot. Once Emilio Zagrep
reunited a whale and a dead lighthouse keeper.

*   *   *

Like any longtime professional
who's entered his field out of empassioned dedication,
I revere (may kid about, but truly revere)
the legendary figures. How many of us
might have the inner capability—I don't know.
Few are given the opportunity
Lorttimer had, or Zagrep, or Mangini. I thought
for days, with a tonic jolt of hubris
adrenalizing my system, that I'd found my chance
at stardom in these dear, disrupted honeymooners
so bent now on disrupting the scene of tragedy
in their turn. The scale was large enough:
a century. The poignancy was about the size
of an opera house or a cruise ship. But
a tragedy is only the sum of its individual tear ducts.
When I spoke with them
—though "spoke" isn't right, and really
"them" is misleading... when we overlapped
our sentiences in the hazeworld, I began to see
how wrong I would be, to use these two

confused, mistreated presences—they were children
really, even throughout their urge toward marital tanglement—
for celebrity's sake. Their story
was simply two people big, was sad and scared
two people big. As if that isn't woefulness and heartache
enough for any of us.

*   *   *

The final time we "overlapped"....
When I was a child, self-secreted
in that ragged-edged viaduct jungle,
I would look out at the ocean
(it was far, but not impossibly so)
and study the massive banks of clouds
that weighed down on the horizon line like a mountain chain.
They looked as if a bullet would bounce straight off them.
Every now and then a cloud extension, genie-like,
would rise by a thin connective wisp
and take its own shape in the blue
—a camel, a submarine, a lady's boobies, an ogre's nose—
but it couldn't maintain integrity
for long, its border would fluctuate,
its core would grow transparent, and finally
the wisp—the part I thought of
as its road back—thinned, then broke,
and there was nothing left but air in the air,
nothing.
I felt that happening to me.
I'd felt it on other cases, but not this
gooseflesh direly, and I was as frightened
—heartstop, drymouth frightened—as anybody
who chatted with ghosts for a living could ever be.
To talk the talk of Samuel and Liza Ruby Williams
in their spirit-essence, I became—a portion of me—

spirit-essence, and in my fascination
with their plight and its current drygoods-flinging devolvement,
I became too much an element of their world,
I was char in sunlight, only char in sunlight
in my mind, my body emptying all the while, going
comatose, and I saw the gossamer tendril
of attachment to my physical life
begin to fray, then further fray, then more,
I was lost, beyond recovering, lost, lost, lost,
fray, snap
   doop doop
She'd seen, and set the beeper on her watch.

        * * *

She'd seen, she'd shrewdly guessed at what was happening,
and pressed her watch's beeper. It was
lifeline back enough.
That night,
when we both went to bed
at a little motel up the road from her office,
I have to admit
the watch, that she set on the bedside table
on top of her pile of undergarments
folded regimentally neat,
was as wondrous to me as the sex itself
—the being here and not elsewhere.

       *

But we *do* know we can use a velocipede,
mounted on several brackets, to churn the butter. We know
that patent number Six-eight-four-two-nine-nine is for
"Home Hygienic Billiards," in which the balls are propelled
across the table by breathing through a tube apparatus,
and this is "conducive to exercise of the lungs." We know
the breath will also warm the feet "which suffer, especially
in winter, by reason of contact with floors and frozen ground,"
and patent number One-eight-six-nine-six-two
offers, therefore, "a simple contrivance," again
of engineered tubes and a mouthpiece. Patented August 2 5, 1 868:
"Improved Burial Case"—essentially a package
containing a ladder and a bell, for the advantage of
the prematurely buried. December 1 3, 1 898:
"Electrical Bedbug Exterminator." Five-eight-seven-nine-nine-four:
"Surgical Appliance" for the prevention
"of involuntary seminal emissions during sleep," by means
of a tucking ring and pricking-points. These
nineteenth century drawings are precise, and love
their diagrammatic letters and numbers showering over
schematic bodies, as if our problems might truly be solved
if only the rain of labels was thick and
explanatory enough, and maybe they're right. Our
feet are cold, our deaths are daily, and about
our lusts and savage attacks of pestiferousness
I will not write, except to say that
all of the ingenuity we can bring to bear upon such terrible peril
is terribly needed. We want to *know*.
We will not fool with hoodoo guesswork,
no; the line between our waking and our sleeping
is a slippery, jagged line, and what we need to persevere is
knowing "weightblock 3 0 vibrates the upper end of arm 2 9-A,
which pushes rod 3 1 backwards," and there you have it:
"Automatic Hat Saluting Mechanism," and many another.

"Seven-Second Rabbit Skinner." "Hands-Free Mop and Window
   Squeegee."
"The Compact Household Information Retrieval Rack," so
"any fact is at fingertip's spin" and we can know
the-state-bird-of, the-exports/imports-of, so we can be prepared
to properly expunge a ketchup stain or to opine upon the Trinity,
we *lust* to know the secrets of the body of a data base.
We want to leave our bite-mark in it. Swedish doctor
Nils-Olof Jacobson placed the beds of terminal patients
on scales, and calculated that twenty-one grams was the average
weight drop at the moment of death:
the weight of the soul. And there you have it.
And now you know.

✳

October 3

Well! Nobody's going to see *this* entry!!!

We met at the warehouse, at 9 p.m. He'd already "cleared the ethe-real bridge," as he put it.

It seemed to me that the dim-lit air of The Gull, and the merchan-dise on the shelves there—rustled. Barely, but rustled. As if in expec-tation. That was the only sign.

We used what equipment the shelves could provide. That was part of the physics, part of the aesthetics, of this transaction, he said—we needed to use what was there, in that building, ghosts "are very cos-mos-bound to their buildings." Okay with me. We'd gone over this rigmarole before, I knew its outline. And it's not as if just then I had anything better to do with my unused stock.

He took a funnel, he placed it into a vial of Holy Water. That was for Samuel Williams. He did the same, right after, for Liza Ruby. There was more of his trance-like mumbojumbo. Mr. Abracadabra. Two scented candles. Fennel, he told me. The air was—pressure air, as if before a storm.

I'd found the hospital hypodermics (what was left of the original shipment, after some fanciful aerial loop-de-loops). He injected him-self from his vial. Then he injected me, from mine.

It was easy enough. On the floor of The Gull, by fennel-light, we made love.

And at last, after one hundred years of waiting, love was being made *through* us.

Long after the candles guttered, we lay there heavily in each other's arms. The air was still. The air seemed to say to me, OPEN FOR BUSINESS. Ribbon cutting. Champagne. Reporters.

The air was calm, and I was calm.

Untenanted by restless spirits.

October 4

Questions:

Can they return? No (he says)
That's a written guarantee? Yes (he says)
Is any of the damage tax deductible? No (Samantha says)
Should we continue to "see each other"? No (we both say) then Yes (we both say) so who knows?
Aren't we married already, in some strange way, for a century?

He gave me, with gestures that seemed to attach a vast importance to it, an old-time rhinestone men's lapel pin. I imagine my eyes said: *So?*

"It's a token," he told me. (*Of what?* But I think I know.) "It was my first—" then he searched a minute for *my* terminology "—intercom system."

✳

postlude

time: 1938
place: the seacoast, where its rock jumble thins to sand;
an elderly man is pensively walking the edge of the water

Nobody knows. Sometimes
it makes me want to giggle like a five-year-old
who's just got away with a stash of prohibited cookies
unobserved. Or maybe five-year-olds today go right
for the cash, who knows? A ten here, twenty there,
it adds up. It added up for me,
once—there was a night at the Royal Palms,
just me and two well-seasoned blondes of Valkyrian stature,
and I filled the clawfoot bathtub completely
with hundred-dollar bills. Go take a dip,
ladies, I said, or I *think* I said, it was so
long ago. Whoever he was, that dandy wiseass of a fellow
with the feather in his hatband, I don't know him anymore.
I'm—look at me! Seventy-five: who *could* be,
just as easily, a ribcage and a rusted knife
overgrown in the woods, like a Dutch still-life
gone morbid. Instead, I walk my skin
of venerable liver-spots into the seaside sun each day
at four o'clock, and I tip my yacht cap
with a frail, but appreciated, worldly charm
to the passing parade of young mothers; my own
gaggle of grandchildren runs to my arms and fills them
like a basket of peaches—so small, so fuzzy and sweet,
etc. (and five-year-olds among them: I could ask
about the cookies-versus-money question,
if I remember: lately, though, the memory is blowing
like confetti out an open window...); and even surface
learning has been made mine (the Dutch painting!

the Valkyries shtick!) and occasionally
a deeper learning—as when I enrolled three years ago
for Talmud class—has touched
a sanctum-place inside me, lighting a tremulous
lamp flame there. Isn't *this*
Respectability with a large, gilt, filigree "R"!
Then why do I think it's really just tinsel and ash,
they *do* know, or they soon will know, I'll give it
all away in some defenseless, confessional moment.
There are voices in my head sometimes
that aren't mine, they coil like a vapor
through my braintwists. What are they saying? The words
stop short of any sense, but their urgency makes me afraid.
One day I'll stand on the beach and shit
my old-man's breeches, and stink in the afternoon breeze,
and the spots on my own skin will arrange themselves
into a brief, denouncing message. One day
my foulness will explode: I'll kneel
in front of my five-year-old granddaughter
and I'll nestle my face on her innocent muff
and yell out who I am. And if not... the world knows,
and the world can bide its time. I've heard the gulls shriek
as they rake the water, calling out
my name that they used at the billiards club and the pony halls
in the days when I could snap a man's small finger
like a match, for laughs, or just to wow
the silk pants off some slinky, winky,
rouged-up downtown dish,
the fish! the fish! the fish!

✳

"CRYSTAL BALL" LAPEL PIN!—for men, or "crystal ball" pendant for ladies! Send us a black and white photo of any friend or relative (up to 8 x 10), we'll turn it into a hologram that, at the touch of a microchip dot, appears in this stylish one-inch-diameter glassite globe. Conduct your own seance! It's a great gag *or* a serious memento. Allow six weeks. State men's or women's version when ordering. Only $15.95. *Gull Gifts.*

diminuendo, with quotes

It's a nothing-sky over Wichita, Kansas.
Invisible cloud, and a few barely-visible stars.
The poet's out for a walk, with nothing to distract him
from himself, his spitting flame-of-a-self
he's brought out to the dark streets of his city
at the close of a poem. Whatever light we give to,
or withhold from, one another—whatever
burning we do—we're larger than the stars,
when it comes right down to our own necessary
perspective. He's been up all night
—it's 5 a.m.—to write, been
"counting wolves," he calls it, forcing himself
awake and—hopefully, anyway—aware.
But then the imp-voice in him rises and asks
who's *he,* to believe his rippled thoughts
and windblown words should be set down on paper?
He knows—what? himself? his wife
asleep upstairs in her familiar sweetcream skin?
But... in the opium den, at the drear start
of *The Mystery of Edwin Drood*, Dickens shows us
people, and maybe by implication everybody,
harboring (as the pop-psych texts would implausibly
nautically phrase it) a secret, inner life, unknowable
except through such extreme release; and even
objects: the opium pipes are made
"of old penny ink-bottles, deary." Everything
drifts in a smoke-gray, purplish *else.* Is it
because of this that Dickens loves his lists
of what's been safely mapped and captioned?
—so, of somebody's almost museumly larder: "The pickles,
in a uniform of rich brown double-vested coat,
announced their portly forms, in printed capitals, as

Walnut, Gherkin, Onion, Cabbage, Cauliflower, Mixed.
The jams announced themselves in feminine calligraphy,
to be Raspberry, Gooseberry, Apricot, Plum, Damson,
Apple, and Peach.... Lowest of all,
a compact leaden vault enshrined the sweet wine
and a stack of cordials: whence issued whispers
of Seville Orange, Lemon, Almond, and Caraway-seed."
These hasty notes he's taken from that same erratic,
incomplete novel. We'll never know
its intended end. Our poet
mumbles some 5 a.m. frustration over this thought.
He's in that awful state of being simultaneously
sleepy and jazzed-up. He's
—me, is who he is. And: *So?*, as one of his characters
recently put it. She walks the beach now
in her own contemplative mutter (although
for her it's afternoon) and idly watches the lapping
cover and uncover the sand—a lace mantilla
peekaboo game. That's all so far
from land-locked me in Kansas, it isn't
a smear of brine, it isn't
even the ghost of a smear of brine, on my horizon.
But I'm off-and-on reading a fantasy novel,
Fletcher Pratt's ornate *The Well of the Unicorn,* and
its shipdeck-and-fishing-village scenes
persuasively offer a second-hand touch of the coastal,
of a river meeting the sea:
"...from the left hand brown Välingsveden swept
to slip his waters almost secretly into the blue."

And so it goes—the great length of what we know,
into what we don't know.

ABOUT THE AUTHOR

Albert Goldbarth is the author of numerous books of poetry, including *Heaven and Earth: a cosmology*, winner of the National Book Critics Circle Award; *Jan. 31*, which was nominated for the National Book Award; and *Across the Layers: Poems Old and New*. He has also published two volumes of personal essays: *Great Topics of the World* (Godine, 1995) and *A Sympathy of Souls*. He lives in Wichita, Kansas.